FLAMENGO

Ronaldinho

FLAMENGO

ODYSSEYS

JIM WHITING / JASON OLSON

CREATIVE EDUCATION · CREATIVE PAPERBACKS

Published by Creative Education and Creative Paperbacks
P.O. Box 227, Mankato, Minnesota 56002
Creative Education and Creative Paperbacks are imprints of
The Creative Company
www.thecreativecompany.us

Design and production by Blue Design (www.bluedes.com)
Art direction by Graham Morgan
Edited by Aidan Whitcomb

Images by Alamy Stock Photo/Art Collection 2, 34–35, Fotoarena, 12, 68, UtCon
Collection, 31; Associated Press/Anonymous, 80, Luciano Belford/AGIF, 8–9,
Sports Press Photo/Sipa USA, cover; Getty Images/ANTONIO SCORZA, 58,
Buda Mendes, 2, 66–67, 77, ERNESTO BENAVIDES, 71, Keystone-
France, 38–39, Lucas Uebel, 61, Matthew Ashton - EMPICS, 4–5,
MB Media, 64, Peter Robinson – EMPICS, 51, 52, Popperfoto, 6,
Print Collector, 28–29, Shaun Botterill, 63, Wagner Meier, 72–73;
Public Domain, 26; Shutterstock/A.RICARDO, 54–55, Travis Green,
81; Wikimedia Commons/Paulo Cunha Rodrigues Junior, 16–17, public domain, 19,
20, 24–25, Public domain / Arquivo Nacional Collection, 44, Stanpv, 11

Library of Congress Cataloging-in-Publication Data
Names: Whiting, Jim, 1943- author. | Olson, Jason, 1981- author.
Title: Flamengo / Jim Whiting and Jason Olson.
Description: Mankato, Minnesota : Creative Education and Creative
   Paperbacks, [2025] | Series: Odysseys in sports: soccer champions |
   Includes bibliographical references and index. | Audience: Ages 12-15 |
   Audience: Grades 7-9 | Summary: "A sports history for teen readers of
   the Brazilian soccer club Flamengo, highlighting the association
   football team's championship cups and the players who helped it achieve
   worldwide fame"– Provided by publisher.
Identifiers: LCCN 2024022757 (print) | LCCN 2024022758 (ebook) | ISBN
   9798889892991 (library binding) | ISBN 9781682776650 (paperback) | ISBN
   9798889894100 (ebook)
Subjects: LCSH: Clube de Regatas do Flamengo–Juvenile literature. | Soccer
   players–Brazil–Biography–Juvenile literature.
Classification: LCC GV943.6.C58 W55 2025 (print) | LCC GV943.6.C58
   (ebook) | DDC 796.334092/2 [B]–dc23/eng/20240525
LC record available at https://lccn.loc.gov/2024022757
LC ebook record available at https://lccn.loc.gov/2024022758

Printed in China

Romario

LEONIDAS

O maior artilheiro do Brasil
(Copa do Mundo — 1938)

Homenagem do Lab. Leão do Norte — Bahia

CONTENTS

Introduction

Soccer, also known as football or fútbol around the globe, is truly a universal game, perhaps the most popular sport in the world. With an estimated 40 million fans around the globe, Rio de Janeiro-based Flamengo is one of the most popular soccer clubs in the world. Also known as the "Rubro-Negro" (Portuguese for red-black), "Mengão" (Big 'Mengo, short for Flamengo) or "Urubu" (Vulture), the club began its rich history first as a rowing club in 1895.

OPPOSITE: José Paolo Guerrero kicks the ball during a match between Flamengo and Botafogo at the Maracana Stadium for the 2017 Brazil Cup.

Originating in Europe, soccer quickly spread to the rest of the world. The governing body Fédération Internationale de Football Association (FIFA) is divided into six confederations. The South American Football Confederation, or CONMEBOL (Confederación Sudamericana de Fútbol), regulates soccer in South America. Nearly every country has at least one league with several divisions. Those divisions are determined by how well, or not well, teams perform in a unique process known as promotion and relegation. At the end of each season, the bottom teams move down a division while the same number of teams move up a division. This creates a consistently high level of competition, especially late in the season among those teams in the promotion/relegation zone.

Flamengo, 1960

Soccer has an often-bewildering array of tournaments. Brazilian teams have several championship opportunities starting at the state level. The two most notable are São Paulo's Campeonato Paulista (nicknamed "Paulistão") and Rio de Janeiro's Campeonato Carioca. Games typically begin in January and continue through April or May. Each team plays all other teams in its level once. The Campeonato Carioca has two stages, the Taça Guanabara and the Taça Rio. The winners of each stage face off for the title. If a team wins both stages, it is declared the champion.

Because of Brazil's vast size and limited transportation, the country did not have a true **national league** until 1959 when the Taça Brasil was formed. It was replaced 10 years later by the Campeonato Brasileiro (commonly "Brasileirão"), which currently consists of 20 teams.

Teams play each other twice in a May to December season. They receive three points for a win, one point for a tie, and no points for a loss. The champion is the team with the most points.

Brazil's national cup tournament, Copa do Brasil, is similar to England's FA Cup. Founded in 1989, it begins with 86 teams representing all 26 Brazilian states as well as the Federal District. Participation is based on state championship results. It is a single-elimination knockout tournament that runs in several phases from March to November.

Continent-wide competitions include CONMEBOL's prestigious Copa Libertadores de América. It dates back to 1960 and is generally regarded as being on a competitive par with Europe's Champions League. It begins with nearly 50 teams and consists of six rounds of competition. The winner also plays in the FIFA Club World Cup. It includes the top teams from each of the six confederations and the host nation. The winner is regarded as world champion.

That Sinking Feeling

In 1889, Brazil's military overthrew the ruling monarch and declared that the country was now a republic. England became the new republic's leading trading partner, and many English people moved there. The newcomers brought many of their customs with them. These customs included sports, especially rowing and cricket. Wealthy young Brazilians eagerly embraced these new activities.

OPPOSITE: *The Proclamation of the Republic*, a painting by Oscar Pereira da Silva, shows the morning of November 15, 1889, in Rio de Janeiro, when Brazil's political system changed from monarchy to republic.

Soccer came to the city of Rio de Janeiro in the late 1800s. A wealthy young man named Oscar Cox returned home after attending school in Lausanne, Switzerland. When he wasn't studying, Cox learned to play soccer. He wanted to add soccer to Rio's list of new sports, so he arranged the first soccer games in the city. In 1901, he took a major step forward. Cox took on a team from Rio to São Paulo, where another Englishman, Charles Miller, had started a team.

Brazil's two most populous states and their respective capital cities were thereby linked. A local newspaper reported approvingly of the game: "The crowd... besides being very select, was very big, and prominent were the elegant women who lent a happy note to the festivities."

Not everyone approved of the sport. "A group of Eng-lishmen, a bunch of maniacs as they all are, get together

Oscar Cox

The Flamengo Rowing Club in 1896

from time to time to kick around something that looks like a bull's bladder," scoffed a Rio newspaper. "It gives them great satisfaction or fills them with sorrow when this kind of yellowish bladder enters a rectangle formed by wooden posts."

Cox shrugged off the criticism. In 1902, he convinced several of his wealthy friends to form a team, which they named Fluminense Football Club. *Flumen* is the Latin word for "river" and refers to the Rio de Janeiro ("River of January"), which is the name Portuguese explorers gave to the area when they arrived in 1502. Those explorers were somewhat mistaken. What they thought was a *rio*, or river, was actually an inlet off the Atlantic Ocean, now called Guanabara Bay. But the name Rio de Janeiro stuck.

Fluminense FC enjoyed success in its early years. It captured the inaugural Campeonato Carioca in 1906 by winning all 10 of its games. It repeated as champion the following three years, losing just a single game in that span. After a runner-up finish in 1910, "Tricolor" (nicknamed for the team colors of red, green, and white) regained the title in 1911 by going undefeated again and allowing just a single goal. Despite this run of success, nine of the 11 players declared their unhappiness with the way the team was being run. They decided to form a new team.

One of the unhappy Fluminense players was Alberto Borgerth. He also belonged to the Flamengo Rowing Club. Flamengo is a district in the city of Rio de Janeiro. It owes its name to a 1599 "invasion" by the Dutch. They landed near modern-day Rio with the intention of securing provisions for what became a round-the-world voyage, by whatever means were necessary. The local Portuguese settlers fought back. At that time the

Portuguese called the Dutch "Flemish," referring to people who lived in an area of Belgium called Flanders. The settlers named the landing site Praia do Flamengo, or "Beach of the Flemish."

Founded on November 17, 1895, the Flamengo Rowing Club was based here. (The club officially celebrates its anniversary two days earlier, to coincide with the national holiday Republic Day.) The new club's members hoped to impress the young women in their

The Flamengo Rowing Club in 1914

neighborhood with their rowing prowess. They nearly never had the chance to do that. When they took their boat out into Guanabara Bay for the first time, strong winds flipped it over. A passing fishing boat rescued the rowers. Despite that rocky start, Flamengo was a thriving organization when Borgerth urged his fellow rowers to accommodate his disgruntled teammates. The rowers agreed, but not unanimously. Some of them thought that soccer was "unmanly." There was a problem with being associated with a rowing club: its property consisted primarily of a boathouse. There were no fields on which to train. So the soccer players practiced on nearby Russel Beach in front of curious onlookers. That may have been the start of Flamengo's reputation as a team of the "common people," in contrast to Fluminense's aristocratic origins.

Flamengo vs. Fluminense, 1912

With almost every former Fluminense starter playing for Flamengo,
the Rubro-Negro romped through their opening three games, scoring
29 goals. So when the teams met for the first time, the 800 fans in
attendance expected Flamengo to dominate. But right from the start,
Fluminense made it clear it had no intention of rolling over. Edward
Calvert opened the scoring in the first minute. Flamengo responded,
and the first half ended 1–1. Seventeen minutes into the second half,
James Calvert beat Flamengo keeper Baena (in white above) and
put the Tricolor ahead again. With two minutes remaining, Flamengo
evened the score. But in the final minute, Bartô put in the game-winner
for Fluminense.

The club's colors were scarlet and black, giving Flamengo its first nickname: "Rubro-Negro." As it began enjoying success, a second nickname was added: "Mengão" (Big Mengo). The team lived up to that future nickname in its very first game on May 3, 1912. Flamengo crushed Sport Club Mangueira 16–2. Right winger Gustavo de Carvalho scored the team's first-ever goal. He put up three more during the rout. Two other players matched his four-goal output. Borgerth added three. To this day, it is the team's most lopsided victory.

Um momento sensacional durante um ataque dos Fl

Fla-Flu

Two months later, the Rubro-Negro played Fluminense for the first time since the split. The atmosphere was festive. According to noted soccer writer Eduardo Galeano, "The boxes were festooned with flowers, fruits, feathers, drooping ladies, and raucous gentlemen. While the gentlemen celebrated each goal by throwing their straw hats onto the playing field, the ladies let their fans fall and collapsed from the excitement of the goal or the oppression of heat and corset."

OPPOSITE: An early Campeonato Carioca game between Flamengo and Fluminense

The gentlemen had several opportunities to fling their hats onto the field. In a major upset, Fluminense defeated Flamengo 3–2.

Flamengo returned the favor three months later, winning 4–0. From that point, it continued to dominate the games between the two teams. Flamengo won six more times, and three other games ended in ties. Fluminense finally won for the second time on December 8, 1916. That win sent the pendulum swinging in the other direction. In the next three years, Fluminense won five times and drew three.

These were the formative years of one of the most storied rivalries in all of soccer. Their games became known as the Clássico das Multidões, or the "Derby of the Masses." In 1925, this rivalry acquired its enduring

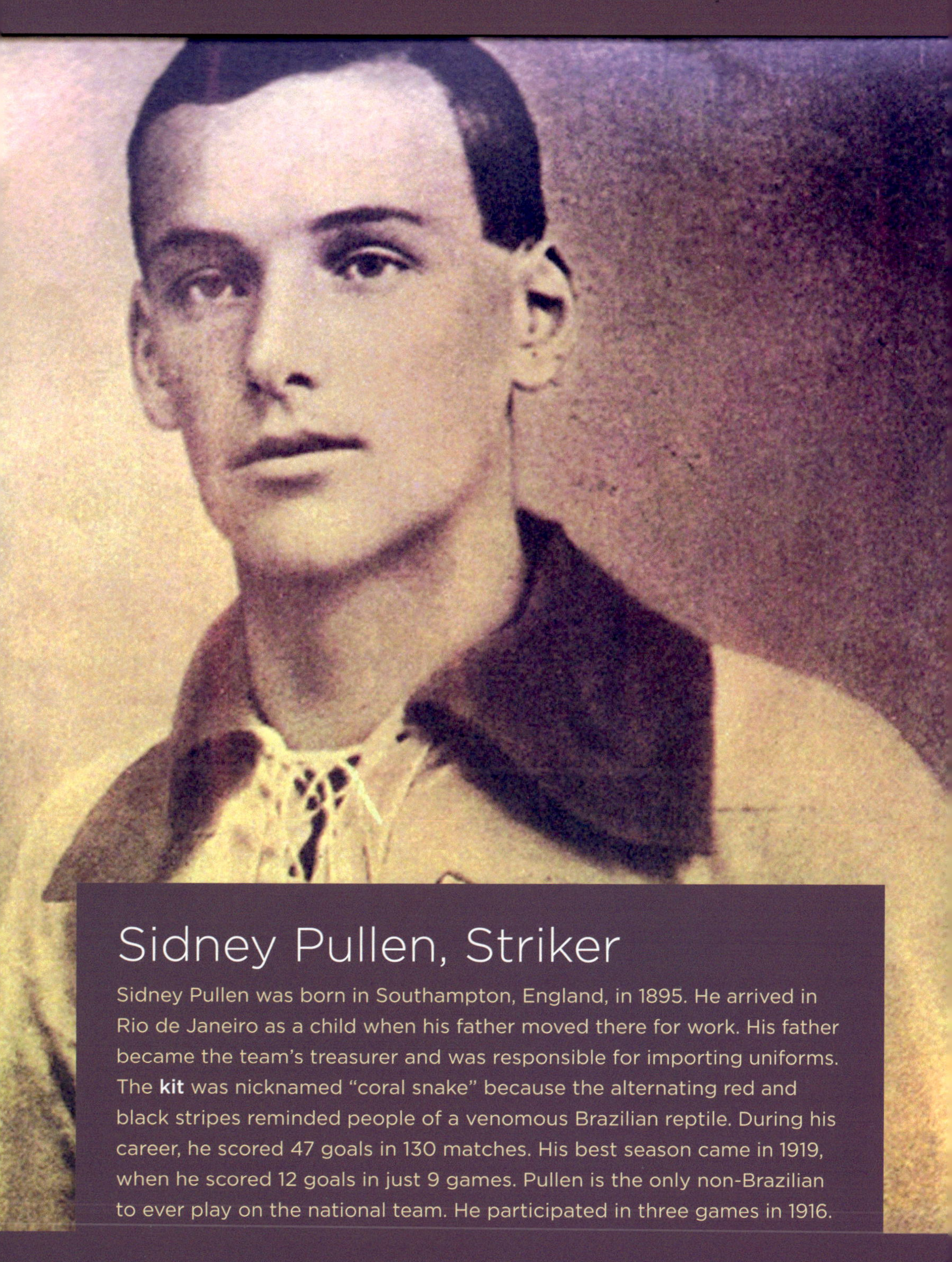

Sidney Pullen, Striker

Sidney Pullen was born in Southampton, England, in 1895. He arrived in Rio de Janeiro as a child when his father moved there for work. His father became the team's treasurer and was responsible for importing uniforms. The **kit** was nicknamed "coral snake" because the alternating red and black stripes reminded people of a venomous Brazilian reptile. During his career, he scored 47 goals in 130 matches. His best season came in 1919, when he scored 12 goals in just 9 games. Pullen is the only non-Brazilian to ever play on the national team. He participated in three games in 1916.

nickname. A young journalist named Mário Filho noted that the Rio de Janeiro side in the Brazilian State Teams Championship was composed entirely of Flamengo and Fluminense players. He referred to it as the "Fla-Flu team." That team went on to win the championship.

Filho's nickname stuck. Thereafter it was applied to the rivalry between the two teams. Since then Fla-Flu has appeared on virtually every list of the top 10 rivalries in the sport of soccer. "Fla-Flu has no beginning. Fla-Flu has no end. Fla-Flu began 40 minutes before time. And then the masses awoke," penned mid-1900s writer Nelson Rodrigues, who was also Filho's brother. "Fla-Flu has become a synonym for rivalry, but it's not like other rivalries. It's not something warlike. Flamengo was born out of Fluminense, so it's more like rivalry between two brothers who know each other very well," added documentary filmmaker Renato Terra, who made a film about the derby. The official FIFA website chimes in with "few other derbies around the world can match the Fla-Flu for historical significance or for its ability to produce dramatic, defining moments."

Some of those moments occur off the field. To many people, Fluminense remains linked to its upper-class, aristocratic origins. Flamengo's status as Brazil's most popular team reflects its broad-based appeal—especially among the country's lower classes. Typically, calling someone a Flamenguista—whether in a soccer context or not—is an insult. It implies that the person lives in one of Rio's many slums. Noted soccer author Alex Bellos writes, "I have met Fluminense fans living in poverty who believe they are more socially refined than their

Rio de Janeiro, late 1800s

Flamenguista neighbors—merely because of their choice of football club."

As of 2024, Flamengo held a slight edge in the number of wins (164–141). With well over 400 games played, nearly a third have ended in ties (145), including a 0–0 draw on March 16, 2024. Fluminense's biggest win over its rival was a 5–1 victory in 1943. Flamengo returned the favor two years later with a 7–0 thrashing. One of the most famous matches came in the 1995 Campeonato Carioca played June 25 at the Maracanã Stadium. Fluminense's Renato Gaucho scored the winning goal off his stomach for the 3–2 final. Fluminense won the stage with 33 points with Flamengo behind by one point, losing on its platinum anniversary (100 years).

Of course, there is much more to Flamengo than Fla-Flu. The team was successful right out of the gate.

In 1913, its first year in the Campeonato Carioca, the Rubro-Negro finished second, just two points from taking the title. They won the championship the next two years. English-born midfielder Sidney Pullen was one of the stars during the team's formative years. Striker Moderato Wisintainer and midfielders Newton Barbosa and Humberto de Araújo Benevenuto kept the team at the top reaches of the Campeonato during the 1920s. They won in 1920, 1921, 1925, and 1927 and were runners-up three other times. The 1925 season was especially significant. Not only did Flamengo defeat Fluminense by a single point, they also won six other championships that year. As soccer continued to grow in popularity, the club earned yet another nickname: "O mais querido do Brasil" ("The most beloved in Brazil").

Becoming Brazil's Beloved

A pivotal moment for Flamengo—and for Brazilian soccer—came during the early 1930s when teams began turning pro. Players were tired of a system that made club owners rich from gate receipts while as amateurs they existed in poverty. Many went to Europe so they could start drawing paychecks. A player named Amílcar Barbuy summed up the situation. As he headed for Italy, he fired a parting shot: "For 20 years I have offered my modest services to Brazilian football. What has happened? The clubs got rich, and I have nothing."

OPPOSITE: Brazil plays Italy in the 1938 World Cup semifinals in Paris, France.

Fluminense had been hit especially hard as a result of the player exodus. They supported the movement toward professionalism in order to retain their better players. If Fluminense was in favor of something, it seemed only natural that Flamengo would be opposed. Club president Rivadávia Meyer said, "The club gives him [the player] all the material necessary to play football and to enjoy himself with the game, and he wants to earn money as well? I will not allow this in Flamengo. Professionalism degrades the man." As it turned out, Meyer wound up being "degraded" himself. Within a few years, Brazilian soccer had become entirely professional.

As Flamengo completed this transition, it also began justifying its O mais querido do Brasil nickname. The club was at the heart of the 1938 movie *Alma e Corpo de uma Raça (The Body and Soul of a Race)*. The main character is Luizinho, a young Flamengo player with big dreams and little money. He lives in the shadow of his dead father, a former star striker, while also scrambling to pay for his medical studies. His childhood sweetheart, Maria Helena, returns from Europe. They rekindle their affection. But Maria Helena's family wants her to marry Rubens, a Flamengo player who comes from a wealthy family. Maria Helena says whoever scores more goals in the season will win her hand. Rubens realizes that Maria doesn't care for him and nobly withdraws from the "competition." Luizinho not only has a successful season on the pitch but also completes his medical studies. That pleases Maria Helena's family. As a doctor, he can provide her with a good living. Flamengo was heavily involved with the production, providing many of the sets and players for the film.

Flamengo was even better in the real world. José Bastos Padilha, the owner of a highly successful printing company, had become club president in 1933. Unlike Meyer, he fully embraced the concept of professionalism. He also recognized that, to be successful in the new world of professional soccer, the team needed to make money. Padilha built the Estádio da Gávea (Gávea Stadium) to accommodate more fans. More importantly, he partnered with Mário Filho, who had just taken over the sports newspaper *Jornal dos Sports*. Filho was an unabashed Flamengo supporter. Rubro-Negro enjoyed almost daily coverage in the newspaper's distinctive pink pages. Live radio broadcasts and an extensive touring schedule took Flamengo to almost every corner of the country. Padilha also hired the country's three leading black players—Fausto dos Santos, Domingos da Guia, and Leônidas da Silva. When Flamengo played Fluminense,

The rivalry between Flamengo and Fluminense is called the "Derby of the Crowds" because of the vast throngs who pass through the turnstiles to witness each game. This nickname was especially fitting when Maracanã Stadium hosted Fla-Flu for the first time with the Campeonato Carioca at stake. At 177,656, the official paid attendance was the highest ever for the derby and among the highest anywhere in the world. According to reliable estimates, at least 16,000 more people managed to elbow their way in without paying. The game itself, though, was hardly a classic. The teams battled to a 0–0 tie. Flamengo won the championship by a single point.

the opposition chanted the racist slur "coal dust." That only increased support for Flamengo among poor Brazilians.

Padilha also began referring to the country's youngsters as "Generation Flamengo." He provided numerous free cultural and sports programs for them. *Jornal dos Sports* sponsored a contest asking children to write sentences that included the words "Flamengo" and "Brazil." The winners included "Flamengo teaches you to love all things about Brazil" and "Flamengo: Brazil's sentinel."

All these moves paid off on the field. Flamengo won the Campeonato Carioca in 1939 for the first time in 12

Zizinho, Attacking Midfielder

Thomaz Soares da Silva joined Flamengo at age 18. Soon known as "Zizinho," he was the team's star attraction for more than a decade. Brazil hosted the 1950 World Cup. In what was regarded as a national disaster, Brazil lost to Uruguay in the championship game. But Zizinho won the Ballon d'Or award as the tournament's best player. An Italian newspaper compared him to Leonardo da Vinci, "creating works of art with his feet on the immense canvas of the Maracanã pitch." Yet for the rest of his life, he refused to answer the phone on July 16, the anniversary of the ill-fated game.

years. Later that year, the club signed future superstar attacking midfielder Zizinho. Flamengo won the Campeonato Carioca again in 1942 and defended the title the following two years. In 1950, the iconic Maracanã Stadium opened. Unfortunately, the primary reason for its construction—celebrating an anticipated World Cup victory—went south as Brazil lost in the championship game 2–1 in front of a record 173,850 spectators. It hosted more than 150,000 people 26 times and 100,000 people 284 times. Renovations ahead of the 2014 FIFA World Cup reduced its capacity to the current sell-out crowd of 73,139. Flamengo and Fluminense own the all-time club record attendance figure of 194,603. It was Flamengo's home for many years (1950–2003, 2006–10, 2013–15, and 2018–present). The team called the Estádio Luso Brasileiro/Ilha do Urubu Stadium home in 2017–18.

Red and
Black = Gold

According to a well-known story, in 1953, Flamengo was in the midst of a championship drought. They hadn't won the Campeonato Carioca since 1944. Then a Catholic priest approached them. If you attend mass and say the rosary before each match, you will win the championship, he told them. They did—and they did. The same thing happened in 1954 and 1955. But Flamengo finished in a tie for third the following year. The players stopped going to mass.

The team rebounded in 1963. It won the title for the first time in eight years and repeated the feat two years later. Players such as forward Edvaldo Alves de Santa Rosa, better known as "Dida," and midfielder Luís Carlos Nunes da Silva, or "Carlinhos," played key roles during this era. Dida's 244 goals marked him as the second leading scorer in Flamengo history, while Carlinhos' virtuoso performances on the pitch and thin, reedy voice earned him the nickname "The Violin."

Flamengo and Brazilian soccer lost a towering figure in 1966. Mário Filho died suddenly and unexpectedly of a heart attack. His brother Nelson eulogized him as the "creator of crowds" because of his key role in making Brazilian soccer a worldwide force. The Maracanã was renamed Estádio Jornalista Mário Filho in his honor, though most people still refer to it as Maracanã.

Five years later, Flamengo's best-ever player began his extraordinary career. Attacking midfielder Arthur Antunes Coimbra was immortalized as "Zico." Within a few years, team management added players such as midfielder Adílio de Oliveira Gonçalves and defender

Leovegildo Lins da Gama Júnior. Flamengo entered what is known as the team's Golden Age.

The Rubro-Negro won the Campeonato Carioca in 1978. It won the Carioca twice the following year when uncertainty regarding the Campeonato Brasileiro resulted in two separate tournaments in Rio. In 1980, Flamengo won its first Campeonato Brasileiro (Brasileirão). Zico scored 21 of his team's 46 goals as it lost just two of 22 matches. Though they fell short in a bid to defend their Brasileirão title early in 1981, they rebounded to win the Campeonato Carioca a few months later.

The march toward greatness continued with the club's first Copa Libertadores title. That triumph led to the single most important match in Flamengo history: the 1981 Intercontinental Cup in Tokyo, Japan. Striker João Batista Nunes scored twice against heavily favored Liverpool (England). Adílio added a third goal, while keeper Raul Plassmann kept a **clean sheet**. Flamengo won 3–0 to claim the title of world champions. "For the

Intercontinental Cup, 1981
Flamengo vs. Liverpool FC

The Intercontinental Cup matched the winners of the European Cup and the Copa Libertadores. Though often surrounded by several opponents, Flamengo star Zico created all of his team's scoring opportunities. In the 12th minute, Zico launched a pass behind the Liverpool defense in front of Nunes for an easy tap-in. About 20 minutes later, Zico lined up to take a free kick. He fired through a last-second opening. The Liverpool goalie could only watch in despair as Adílio sent the deflection into the net. Then, four minutes before halftime, Zico fired a pass to Nunes, who hit the back of the net to make the score 3–0 and take the victory from the European giants.

Zico, Attacking Midfielder

When Arthur Antunes Coimbra was only 14, a reporter saw him score nine goals in a game. He told Zico's father to take him to Flamengo. He was already a Flamengo fan. Zico was not just the best player during Flamengo's Golden Age, he was the team's best player—period. His 508 career goals are more than twice as many as runner-up Dida, who had 244. He is regarded as one of the best playmakers in history, with an almost uncanny ability to visualize the field. In 1999, Zico placed eighth in the vote for the FIFA Player of the Century.

captain, Zico, 1981 was the year he was confirmed as the planet's top footballer," said *World Soccer*. "His creative and goal-scoring genius allied to Flamengo's other stellar cast members, and their will to succeed helped propel the Brazilians to legendary status."

Flamengo won Brasileirão again in 1982 and 1983. Then Zico left the team to play in Italy, which effectively brought the Golden Age to an end. He returned in 1986 and played several more years. He helped Flamengo to another Carioca title in 1986 and to the 1987 Copa União. A one-off tournament among Brazil's largest and most popular teams, the Copa União was thrown together when the Campeonato Brasileiro was abruptly canceled for financial reasons. Zico made his final appearance at the Maracanã in 1990. Popular Brazilian singer Jorge Ben Jor wrote a popular song, "Camisa 10 da Gávea," about Zico. The "10" refers to his jersey number.

CARIOCÃO GUARAVITON
Guaravita
CAIXA

Keeping the Ball Rolling

Flamengo continued at a high level even without its best-ever player. It won the second Copa do Brasil in 1990 and three more Campeonato Carioca titles in 1991, 1996, and 1999. Flamengo also captured the short-lived Copa de Oro, a CONMEBOL competition that gave the Rubro-Negro its third official international trophy. One of the key players during the latter part of the century was striker Romário de Souza Faria. Romário came to Flamengo in 1995 after being named FIFA World Player of the Year the previous year.

OPPOSITE: Flamengo players lift the cup after winning the Campeonato Carioca in 2014.

The first few years of the 21st century provided a study in contrasts. Flamengo continued to dominate the Campeonato Carioca. Yet it had significant financial issues that resulted in near-relegation from the Campeonato Brasileiro on several occasions, largely because of not being able to attract high-priced talent. The team once avoided relegation only by winning the season's final game.

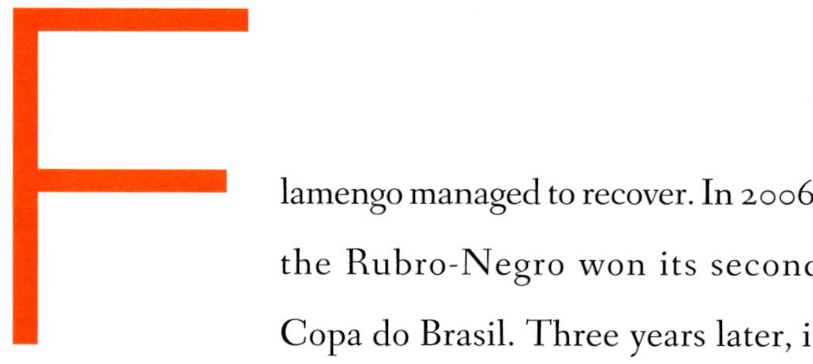

lamengo managed to recover. In 2006, the Rubro-Negro won its second Copa do Brasil. Three years later, it completed its rise from near-relegation to capture its fifth Brasileirão championship. Coupled with three straight Rio championships in 2007, 2008, and 2009, Flamengo was on a roll. Team executives wanted to continue this run of success. A series of complicated negotiations resulted in the high-profile signing of Ronaldinho after a decade in Europe, during which he was twice named FIFA World Player of the Year. "We are pleased to announce the hiring of Ronaldinho for the next four years," said Flamengo president Patricia Amorim in January 2011.

The move paid immediate dividends. A month and a half after suiting up for the Rubro-Negro, Ronaldinho curled a long free kick in over the wall of players to beat Boavista 1–0. That gave Flamengo the Taça Guanabara, which in turn led to the Campeonato Carioca title two months later. But the following year, Ronaldinho claimed

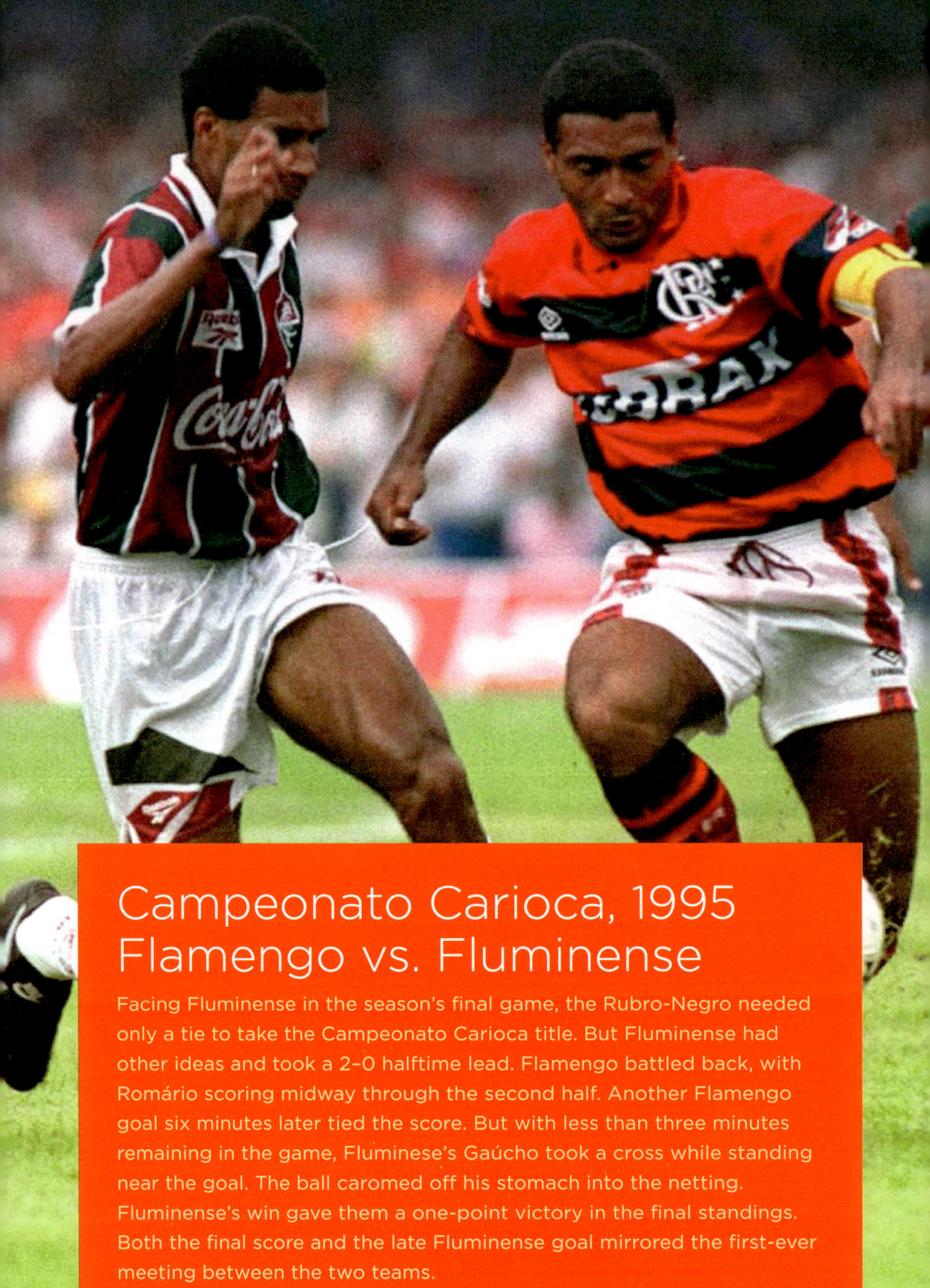

Campeonato Carioca, 1995
Flamengo vs. Fluminense

Facing Fluminense in the season's final game, the Rubro-Negro needed only a tie to take the Campeonato Carioca title. But Fluminense had other ideas and took a 2–0 halftime lead. Flamengo battled back, with Romário scoring midway through the second half. Another Flamengo goal six minutes later tied the score. But with less than three minutes remaining in the game, Fluminese's Gaúcho took a cross while standing near the goal. The ball caromed off his stomach into the netting. Fluminense's win gave them a one-point victory in the final standings. Both the final score and the late Fluminense goal mirrored the first-ever meeting between the two teams.

he hadn't been paid for several months. He left Flamengo in a huff and eventually signed with Fluminense. Even without Ronaldhino, Flamengo hoped for a major championship in 2012, the 100th anniversary of the soccer team's founding. While that didn't happen, the Rubro-Negro claimed its third Copa do Brasil a year later and the Campeonato Carioca in 2014.

The 2017 season is remembered for Flamengo playing in two major finals at the end of the season but not winning either. They lost the Copa do Brasil final in a shootout to Cruzeiro. Three months later, they reached the Copa Sudamericana final but lost to Independiente, with an away loss and a 1–1 draw at home. A mob of Flamengo supporters rioted outside the hotel where Independiente was staying. Flamengo was punished by CONMEBOL with two closed-door home matches in the following Copa Libertadores.

The club added striker José Paolo Guerrero—the first player from Peru to be nominated for the FIFA Ballon d'Or award as Player of the Year, in 2015. In 2017, he

scored both goals in a 2–1 semifinal win over Botafogo in the Campeonato Carioca. Guerrero added another goal in the second leg of the final against none other than Fluminense in the Maracanã for the 3–1 win on **aggregate**. He became the oldest Peruvian player to appear in a FIFA World Cup match as a 34-year-old striker in 2018. His route to the World Cup took many twists and turns after testing positive for a banned substance called benzoylecgonine. A one-year ban from FIFA was the initial punishment, but a Swiss Federal Tribunal lifted the ban six months later.

Looking to end a nine-year Campeonato Brasileiro title drought, Flamengo set a club record for the most weeks in the lead (13) and set a new points record (72) but finished runner-up behind Palmeiras. That season also marked a new era for the club, recording the two highest outgoing transfer fees in club history when 16-year-old Vinicius

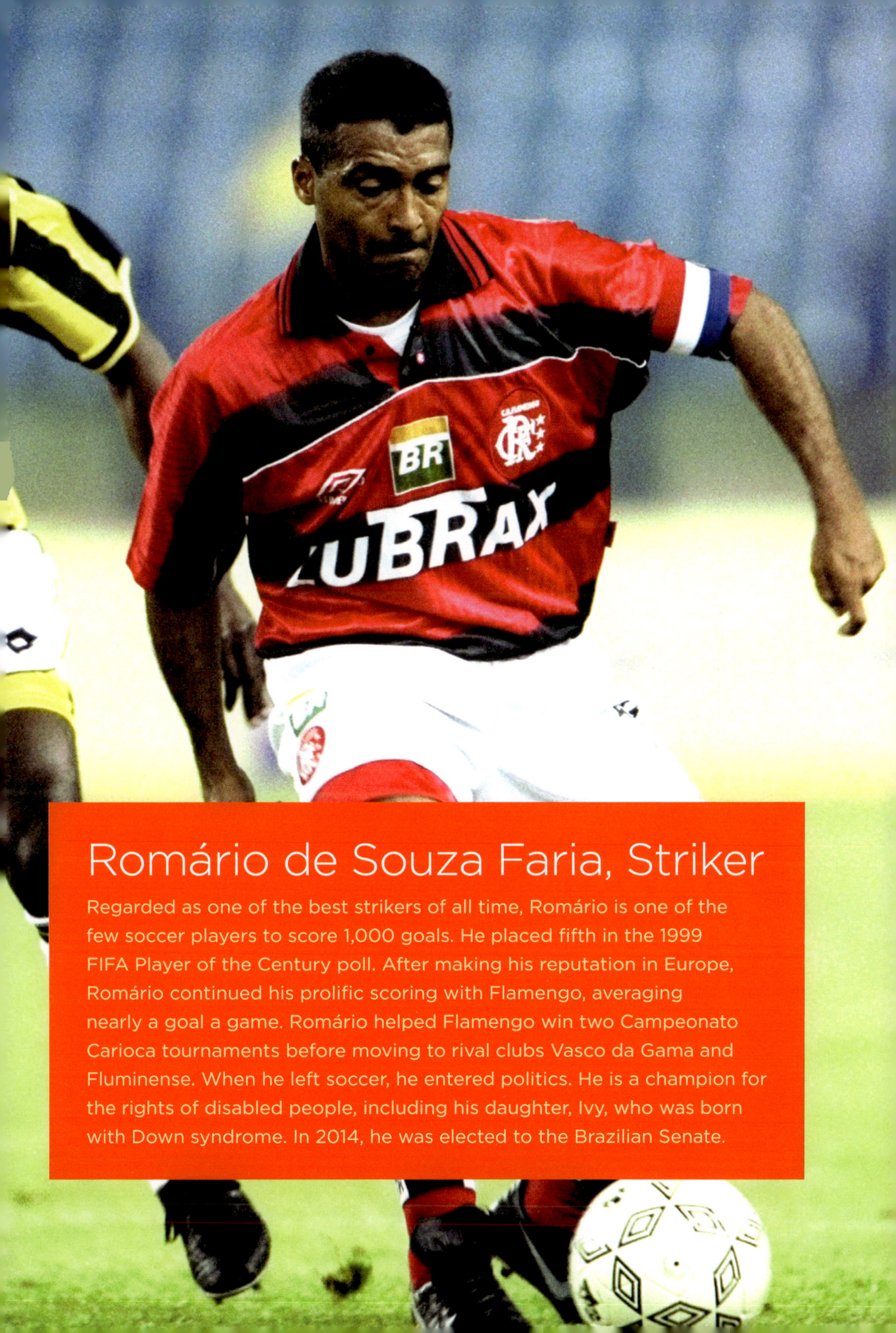

Romário de Souza Faria, Striker

Regarded as one of the best strikers of all time, Romário is one of the few soccer players to score 1,000 goals. He placed fifth in the 1999 FIFA Player of the Century poll. After making his reputation in Europe, Romário continued his prolific scoring with Flamengo, averaging nearly a goal a game. Romário helped Flamengo win two Campeonato Carioca tournaments before moving to rival clubs Vasco da Gama and Fluminense. When he left soccer, he entered politics. He is a champion for the rights of disabled people, including his daughter, Ivy, who was born with Down syndrome. In 2014, he was elected to the Brazilian Senate.

Matheus Gonçalves Martins

Junior signed with Real Madrid for €46 million ($49 million) and 20-year-old Lucas Paqueta signed with AC Milan for €35 million ($37 million). Both developed in the youth academy.

n 2024, Flamengo won its 38th Carioca title, five more than Fluminese on the all-time list. Flamengo and Fluminese have dominated the Carioca in recent years. Flamengo won three consecutive Rio league titles (2019–21) before Fluminese captured the last two titles (2022–23) after being runner-up in 2017, 2020, and 2021. Flamengo was runner-up in 2022 and 2023.

Silent Tribute

One way football clubs honor the memory of those who have passed away is to remain silent at a symbolic time in the match. On February 8, 2019, a fire at the Flamengo training center took the lives of 10 Flamengo youth players aged 14 to 17. The cause was a faulty air conditioner unit that caught fire inside one of the players' rooms at 5 a.m. Flamengo president Rodolfo Landim described it as the worst tragedy the club had experienced in 123 years.

OPPOSITE: Players of Flamengo and Fluminense take a minute of silence in honor of the 10 young athletes who died in a fire at the Flamengo training center on February 8, 2019.

The governor of Rio de Janeiro called for three days of mourning. During the 10th minute of every home match, Flamengo fans sing in the memory of the young people, known as "Garotos do Ninho" (Nest Boys).

The season turned out to be Flamengo's most prolific on the pitch. The club captured the Copa Libertadores

"THE SEASON TURNED OUT TO BE FLAMENGO'S MOST PROLIFIC ON THE PITCH."

on November 23, 2019, in a dramatic 2-1 victory over defending champion River Plate. It was the first single-game final played at a neutral site in Lima, Peru. Gabriel Barbosa, who was moved from AC Milan to Flamengo via a loan during the January transfer window, scored twice in the final minute. In addition to adding Gabriel, the club signed Bruno Henrique from Brazilian foe Santos. Less than 24 hours later, Flamengo won the Campeonato Brasileiro Serie A for the first time since 2009 with four matches to go. It became only the second Brazilian club to win their state championship, Brasileiro, and Copa Libertadores in the same season since Pele's 1962 Santos squad.

Manager Jorge Jesus joined the club after it advanced out of the Copa Libertadores group stage and set several Campeonato Brasileiro's 20-team double round robin era records: most points (90), most wins (28), most goals scored (86), best **goal differential** (+49), longest undefeated streak (24 matches), most points clear of runner-up (16), and most goals scored by a single player (25 by Gabriel). Flamengo capped

Bruno Henrique

Gabriel Barbosa

off the year by participating in the FIFA Club World Cup in Qatar, beating Saudi club Al Hilal SFC 3–1 in the semifinal before falling to Liverpool 1–0 in the final. Brazilian Roberto Firmino's extra-time goal lifted Liverpool to the title as they avenged a 1981 3–0 defeat.

Success continues at the club despite a revolving manager door after Jesus returned to Benfica in July 2020 after winning the revived Supercopa do Brasil and Recopa Sudamericana. Domenec Torrent briefly took over before Rogerio Ceni took over in November 2020. Ceni led the team to a successful Campeonato Brasileiro title, finishing one point ahead of Internacional, and a third title in 2021. He was released after losing four of the opening 10 matches the next season before Renato Gaucho took the team back to the Copa Libertadores final losing to Palmeiras 2–1 in extra time on November

27, 2021. Gaucho and the club parted ways afterward in favor of Paulo Sousa.

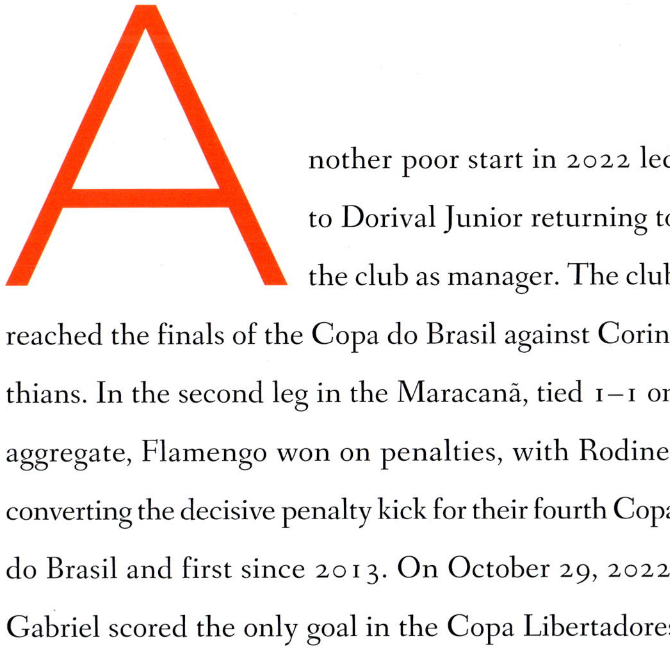

Another poor start in 2022 led to Dorival Junior returning to the club as manager. The club reached the finals of the Copa do Brasil against Corinthians. In the second leg in the Maracanã, tied 1–1 on aggregate, Flamengo won on penalties, with Rodinei converting the decisive penalty kick for their fourth Copa do Brasil and first since 2013. On October 29, 2022, Gabriel scored the only goal in the Copa Libertadores final against Athletico Paranaense in Ecuador to give Flamengo its second Copa Libertadores title in four years and third overall. Tite, Brazil's national team manager in 2016–22, became the Flamengo manager in October 2023 after the national team exited the 2022 World Cup in the quarterfinals, on penalties to Croatia. Tite began coaching in 1990 after playing 11 seasons as a midfielder.

There's little doubt that Flamengo is one of the most significant and enduring soccer teams not only in Brazil but throughout the world. It's one of just two Brazilian teams that have never been relegated. The other is fellow giant São Paulo. The team claims more than 40 million supporters in Brazil alone and uncounted millions more throughout the world.

Diego Ribas da Cunha

Selected Bibliography

Bellos, Alex. *Futebol: The Brazilian Way of Life*. Rev. ed. New York: Bloomsbury, 2014.

Bocketti, Gregg. *The Invention of the Beautiful Game: Football and the Making of Modern Brazil*. Gainesville: University Press of Florida, 2016.

Dempsey, Luke. *Club Soccer 101: The Essential Guide to the Stars, Stats, and Stories of 101 of the Greatest Teams in the World*. New York: W.W. Norton, 2014.

Galeano, Eduardo. *Soccer in Sun and Shadow*. Translated by Mark Fried. New York: Nation Books, 2013.

Goldblatt, David. *Futebol Nation: The Story of Brazil Through Soccer*. New York: Nation Books, 2014.

Goldblatt, David, and Johnny Acton. *The Soccer Book: The Sport, the Teams, the Tactics, the Cups*. 3rd ed. New York: DK, 2014.

Glossary

aggregate   the combined goals scored in a two-game (home and away) series

clean sheet   when a goalkeeper does not give up a goal for the entirety of the game

confederation   an organization which consists of a number of groups

derby	a rivalry between two clubs, typically between neighbors in the same city
goal differential	the difference in goals scored versus goals conceded, which is one of the criteria used to break a tie in the table
kit	team uniforms
national league	a series of interconnected leagues for football clubs within a nation
relegation	when a team moves down a league based on a previous season's performance
transfer window	a period during the off-season when teams are allowed to buy and sell players for their team

Websites

Goal Renato Gaúcho - Goal of the Belly - 1995
https://www.youtube.com/watch?v=coFqyuSUPwo
This short video shows Gaúcho's famous 1995 "belly goal" against Flamengo from several angles.

Zico - 65 Goals for Flamengo in 6 minutes (1973–1989)
https://www.youtube.com/watch?v=qm_BK0LBrbw
Watch 65 of Zico's 500+ Flamengo goals, including a number of the curving free kicks that made him a master of the technique.

Index